MEN-AT-AR

EDITOR: MART

Napoleon's Egyptian Campaigns 1798-1801

Text by MICHAEL BARTHORP

Colour plates by G. A. EMBLETON

OSPREY PUBLISHING LONDON

Published in 1978 by
Osprey Publishing Ltd
59 Grosvenor Street, London W1X 9DA
© Copyright 1978 Osprey Publishing Ltd
Reprinted 1990

ISNB 0 85045 126 4

Filmset by BAS Printers Limited,
Over Wallop, Hampshire
Printed in Hong Kong

Introduction

The imaginative strategic plan of Revolutionary France to cut Britain's lifeline to India by seizing Egypt and the Levant was an epic adventure, set amongst some of the most ancient places of history, then almost unknown to Europeans. It occurred at a critical period both for France and in the fortunes of Napoleon Bonaparte. It failed; yet Bonaparte emerged from it as the chief power in France and in a position to conclude the Revolutionary Wars to his advantage. Nevertheless, it proved once again the supremacy of the British fleet and furthermore that a reformed British Army was a force to be reckoned with in the future.

The aim of this book is to provide an outline of the campaigns and to examine in greater detail the armies which marched and fought amid the desert sands and the relics of earlier civilisations. For the full story, a select bibliography is provided.

CHRONOLOGY OF EVENTS

1793

1 February	Revolutionary France, already at war with Austria and Prussia, declares war on Britain and Holland.

1795

July	France defeats Allies in the Low Countries. Prussia makes peace.
October	The Directory established in France.

1796–97

	General Napoleon Bonaparte's victorious campaign against Austria in northern Italy. Austria makes peace.

1798

February	Bonaparte advises against invasion of England and recommends seizure of Malta and Egypt to cut off Britain's trade with India. Egypt nominally part of Turkish Empire but in effect ruled by Mameluke Beys, Murad and Ibrahim.
19 May	Bonaparte sails with Army of the Orient from Toulon.
12 June	Malta captured.
2 July	French land in Egypt and capture Alexandria.
3 July	Advance on Cairo begins. Murad Bey leaves Cairo to intercept French.
13 July	First action against Murad at Shubra Khit. Mamelukes withdraw and advance continues.
21 July	Battle of the Pyramids. French defeat Murad. Ibrahim Bey on

The Theatre of Operations.

General Napoleon Bonaparte in Egypt; engraving after the painting by Gros. (Anna S. K. Brown Military Collection, Providence, Rhode Island)

	east bank of Nile not engaged. Murad flies south, Ibrahim towards Sinai.
24 July	Bonaparte enters Cairo.
1–2 August	Battle of the Nile. British fleet under Nelson defeats French fleet in Aboukir Bay. British blockade of Egypt follows.
11 August	Bonaparte defeats Ibrahim at Salalieh. Ibrahim flies to Syria. French administration of Egypt begins.
25 August	General Desaix leaves Cairo for Upper Egypt to begin nine-month campaign in pursuit of Murad.
9 September	Turkey declares war on France.
7 October	Desaix's action at El Lahun.
22 October	Rebellion in Cairo crushed.
November–December	(a) Bubonic plague, Egypt. Murad reinforced from Arabia.
	(b) Second Coalition of Britain, Russia, Turkey, Austria and Naples begins to form. The Directory unable to reinforce Bonaparte.
	(c) Bonaparte learns of two Turkish armies forming for invasion of Egypt and of Tippoo Sahib's rising against British in India. he determines to invade Syria to forestall Turkish invasion and deny use of Syrian ports to British fleet.
1799 January–May	Desaix's campaign continues along Upper Nile. Sends Belliard to capture Kosseir on Red Sea.
6 February	Bonaparte begins invasion of Syria.
9–19 February	Siege of El Arish.
7 March	French assault on Jaffa. Bonaparte slaughters 4,000 Turkish prisoners. French attacked by plague.
15 March	Commodore Sir Sydney Smith RN arrives off Acre and organises its defence.
18 March	Bonaparte besieges Acre.
28 March	First assault fails.
April	Main Turkish army reported around River Jordan. Kléber sent to reconnoitre.
16 April	Battle of Mount Tabor. Kléber defeats Turks.
1–10 May	Attacks against Acre continue unsuccessfully.
20 May	Bonaparte raises siege and withdraws to Egypt.
29 May	Belliard captures Kosseir, cutting off Murad's reinforcements from Arabia. Upper Egypt now pacified but Murad still free.
May–June	(a) Successful Russo-Austrian offensive against French in Europe.
	(b) British defeat Tippoo Sahib in India.
14 June	Bonaparte returns to Cairo. Makes secret plans for his own

	return to France.		and Cape of Good Hope under General Baird.
14 July	Turkish army, supported by Anglo-Turkish fleet, lands at Aboukir.	24 November	Abercromby assembles at Malta.
24 July	Bonaparte concentrates his army near Aboukir.	28 November	Austrians defeated at Hohenlinden and make peace.
25 July	Battle of Aboukir. Bonaparte routs Turks. Learns of French defeats in Europe and political crisis in France.	December	Bonaparte persuades Russia to close Baltic to British trade and consider joint plan for attacking India.
23 August	Bonaparte sails secretly for France, leaving Kléber in command in Egypt.	20 December	Abercromby sails for Marmorice Bay near Rhodes to prepare for invasion of Egypt. General John Moore at Jaffa to coordinate operations with Turks.
September–December	(a) French defeat Russians in Switzerland and Anglo-Russian force in Holland. (b) Kléber opens peace negotiations with Turks. (c) New Turkish army advances to El Arish. (d) 9–10 November. 'Coup d'état' of Brumaire. Consulate replaces Directory with Bonaparte as First Consul.	1801 22 February	British sail from Marmorice Bay.
		8 March	Landing at Aboukir Bay. Moore defeats Friant and establishes beachhead.
1800 28 January	Kléber signs treaty with Turks undertaking to evacuate Egypt. Turks advance on Cairo.	12 March	British advance on Alexandria. Menou leaves Cairo for Alexandria with 6,000 reinforcements, leaving Belliard in command.
18 March	Kléber informed British would not recognise treaty. Turks approaching Cairo.	13 March	Battle of Mandora. French withdraw into Alexandria; joined by Menou on 19 March.
20 March	Battle of Heliopolis. Kléber defeats Turks who incite revolt in Cairo.	21 March	Battle of Alexandria (Canope). Menou attacks Abercromby but defeated and withdraws into Alexandria. Abercromby mortally wounded, succeeded by General Hely-Hutchinson.
27 March	French operations to subjugate Cairo, continuing until 22 April.	25 March	One Turkish force lands at Aboukir while another advances from Syria.
May	British land force under General Sir Ralph Abercromby sent to Mediterranean to operate in support of Austria.	1 April	Baird sails from India.
		2 April	British capture Rosetta.
		13 April	French in Alexandria isolated by flooding of Lake Mareotis.
May–June	Austrians defeated at Marengo and Ulm.	26 April	General Coote left to invest Alexandria. Hutchinson and Turks from Aboukir begin advance up Nile.
14 June	Kléber assassinated in Cairo. Menou takes command.		
5 September	British capture Malta.		
October	Britain plans attack on Egypt by Abercromby's army, supported by Turks plus force from India	May–June	Baird arrives at Kosseir and joined by force from Cape.
		9 May	Action at Rahmaniya. French

	forced to withdraw, thus losing communications between Alexandria and Cairo. Turkish Syrian army advancing up east bank of Nile.
19 June	Baird begins advance across desert to Keneh.
21 June	Hutchinson and Turks invest Cairo.
27 June	Belliard, with 13,000 troops, surrenders in Cairo.
15 July	French leave Cairo for Rosetta escorted by Moore. Baird learns of surrender and advances down Nile.
30 July	Moore reaches Rosetta. Belliard's force embarked for France.
9 August	Hutchinson begins operations against Alexandria.
30 August	Menou surrenders. Embarks for France 14 September. Egypt now clear of French troops.
1 October	Peace signed between Britain and France.

The French Army

In 1791 the new rulers of Revolutionary France appreciated that the regular army inherited from the Bourbons would need to be sizeably increased if the achievements of the Revolution were to be maintained and defended from outside interference. Appeals for volunteers and a liability for front-line service imposed on part of the National Guard failed to produce the numbers required, and it was not until July 1792, with Austrian and Prussian armies massing on the eastern frontiers of France, that large numbers of the new levies – known as *fédérés* – came forward in response to the cry of '*La Patrie en danger*'. Without discipline or training, antagonistic to the volunteers of 1791 and disdained by the regulars, the *fédérés*, with only enthusiasm to sustain them, formed the bulk of the army which defeated the Prussians at Valmy and the Austrians at Jemappes in 1792. The danger past however, many of the *fédérés* deserted so that, by 1793, with Britain and other monarchies joining the First Coalition, and the army weakened by the defection of many officers led by General Dumouriez, the victor of Valmy, fresh measures were needed to meet the crisis. A *levée en masse* in August 1793 made all males between 18 and 25 liable for military service, an arrangement which was for-

Battle of the Nile, after the painting by N. Pocock. The British fleet is attacking from the right. (National Maritime Museum)

Battle of the Pyramids. Bonaparte can be seen sheltering in one of the divisional squares, with a *demi-brigade légère* and dismounted dragoons in the foreground. Detail from the painting by General Lejeune. (Cliché des Musées Nationaux, Paris)

mally converted into a Conscription Law in September 1798.

To ameliorate the lack of experience of the early conscript regiments in 1792, it was decided, shortly before Valmy, to break up the old three-battalion regular regiments and to form new units, known as 'demi-brigades', each consisting of one regular and two *fédéré* battalions. This system was adopted for the whole French army in 1794 and by 1798, when the Egyptian campaign began, the demi-brigades had been forged by the campaigning of the intervening years into homogeneous units of tough, experienced conscripts, the squabbles and differences between regulars and volunteers now being things of the past. Some of the officers had held commissions in the Royal army but most were of a new breed hitherto largely unknown in European armies, being men who had risen from the ranks by merit.

The Infantry

The infantry demi-brigades were of two types: line and light infantry, each consisting of three bat-

talions. All were designated simply by a number, with no territorial or other affiliations, as had been the case in the Royal army. A line battalion had one grenadier and eight fusilier companies, the former having a strength of 90 men and the latter about 120 each, giving a battalion strength of around 1,050. Thus a demi-brigade had a notional strength of about 3,000, although in the field the actual number of bayonets seldom reached this figure. The disembarkation strengths of the line demi-brigades forming the Army of the Orient averaged about 1,700 each, the strongest, the 13th, having 2,430 while the 88th only mustered 1,500. The grenadier company was the élite of the battalion, forming the head of a column or providing a flank guard or a reserve when the battalion was formed in line, and its men were selected for their soldierly qualities rather than their size. In the light infantry the *carabinier* company fulfilled the same func-

Battle of Sediman or El Lahun, fought by Desaix's division against Murad Bey, 7 October 1798; engraving after Naudet. (Anna S. K. Brown Military Collection, Providence, Rhode Island)

tions as the grenadiers and the battalion was completed by seven *chasseur* companies. As their name implies, the light battalions had the tasks of providing advance guards and skirmishing screens but would also be expected to fight in the main line of battle with the line battalions.

Four of the five infantry divisions of the Army of the Orient were composed of one light and two line demi-brigades, the battalions of which were organised on the above establishment. Once in Egypt, the need to provide garrisons and other detachments often meant that a demi-brigade would lose one battalion, or part of it. For example, during the expedition to Syria in 1799 seven of the line demi-brigades had to leave their third battalions for the garrisoning of Egypt, while at the Battle of Alexandria in 1801 one of the grenadier companies of the 25th Line was detached to a different division and the 2nd Light was only represented by one *carabinier* company. After the Syrian adventure, due to casualties from action and disease and the inability of any reinforcements to reach Egypt, it was no longer possible to maintain battalions at their full establishment and an order of

27 June 1799 reduced each battalion to one élite and four other companies. The same order specified that the grenadier companies were to be kept at a strength of one captain, one lieutenant, two sub-lieutenants, a sergeant-major, four sergeants, a *caporal-fourrier*, eight corporals, two drummers and seventy grenadiers. In addition, each demi-brigade was to have a company of '*éclaireurs*' (scouts) of three squads, one from each battalion.

Apart from the demi-brigades, there were included 300 *Guides à Pied* and a *Légion Nautique*, formed from sailors, as headquarters troops. During the occupation of Malta in June 1798 a somewhat reluctant *Légion Malte* of just under 400 men was formed to accompany the Army to Egypt. Both the sailors and Maltese were subsequently distributed among the demi-brigades, the artillery and the engineers. In view of the difficulty of obtaining reinforcements from France due to the British naval blockade (although a detachment of the 51st Line did reach Egypt in March 1801), some use was made of locally enlisted men. During the operations by Desaix's division in Upper Egypt between August 1798 and May 1799, 300 men were enlisted into the 21st Light, and in Lower Egypt Kléber, in 1800, formed *Légions* of Copts and Greeks.

Uniforms are examined in greater detail below but, in essentials, the universal home service dress of the infantry, in which the troops landed in July 1798, consisted of a bicorne hat, the blue cut-away coat, or *habit*, with red collar and cuffs, white waistcoat and breeches and long black gaiters. The light infantry coat had minor differences of cut and was worn with blue waistcoat and breeches and calf-length white gaiters. Each demi-brigade was distinguished solely by its number on the buttons. Although some illustrations show the élite companies wearing their bearskin caps, these would seem inappropriate for the desert in mid-summer, and it is more likely that these companies wore bicornes with the falling plumes of red horse-hair detached from the bearskins.

When the Army reached Cairo at the end of July 1798, the infantry's coats were so ragged and had proved so unsuitable in the heat that Bonaparte, on 7 August, ordered cotton clothing to be made up, consisting of a *habit-veste* dyed with indigo, which was to button straight down the front to cover the abdomen, and white gaiter-trousers. The latter proved unsatisfactory and were replaced from 1 October by trousers of unbleached linen, those of the light infantry being dyed blue, and half-gaiters. Since the blue cotton coats would provide insufficient warmth in the cold desert nights, cotton greatcoats of the same colour as the trousers were ordered on 21 September. The new dress, all of which was manufactured by local craftsmen, was completed by a novel headdress, as specified in an order of 13 September: a peaked cap, or helmet, made of sheep's hide dyed black with folding flaps to protect the ears and the back of the neck, and surmounted by a woollen crest, or *pouffe*, dyed in different colours for each demi-brigade. The tricolour cockade was fixed to the left side and, for the élite companies, a grenade on each flap. It was in this uniform that the Syrian campaign was conducted.

The cotton uniforms proving insufficiently hard-wearing, a third uniform, this time of cloth, was devised shortly before Bonaparte himself left for France. The new dress was promulgated by Kléber on 1 October 1799. Since enough blue cloth to clothe the infantry was not available in the country, each demi-brigade was to receive *habit-vestes* in its own individual colour with contrasting facings, thus producing a diverse and impressive effect which, according to an eyewitness, made the army appear more numerous than it really was. The leather caps continued in use and both line and light infantry had trousers of unbleached linen and short gaiters. Officers' coats had long skirts and it would appear that generally they retained the bicorne, as indeed did the élite companies of some *demi-brigades*, e.g. the 9th and 88th Line. The officers' breeches or trousers matched those of the

Battle of Aboukir, 25 July 1799. The French are shown still wearing their 1798 uniforms. Drawing by Duplessis-Bertaux. (Anna S. K. Brown Military Collection, Providence, Rhode Island)

men (although green was worn by the 9th and possibly others) and were worn with Hessian-type boots. This was the uniform worn during the 1801 campaign against the British. (See details below.)

The firearm of the infantryman was the 1777 model Gribeauval musket with 380mm triangular socket bayonet. The NCOs and grenadiers of the line also had a short sword, or *sabre-briquet*, of the 1790 model carried by all enlisted ranks of the light infantry. Grenadier and all light infantry officers were armed with a sabre while those of the fusiliers had a straight sword, though in Egypt this was often exchanged for a sabre. An order issued by Bonaparte on 8 October 1798 required all light infantry lieutenants, sub-lieutenants, and NCOs above the rank of corporal to provide themselves with a carbine or short musket. The infantryman was accoutred with a cow-hide knapsack and an ammunition pouch shoulder belt to which was fitted, for fusiliers only, an attachment for the bayonet; troops armed with the *sabre-briquet* carried them, with the bayonet, on a separate shoulder belt over the right shoulder.

The British landing at Aboukir Bay. In the left background Moore's Reserve is storming the French defences. Detail of an engraving after P. J. de Loutherbourg. (National Army Museum)

Demi-Brigade Dress Distinctions, 1798–1801

It is difficult to state categorically the colours worn, firstly because there were, due to production problems, variations between what was ordered and what was actually made up, and secondly because of the inherent difficulties of describing colours, which in this case are aggravated by problems of translation. The colours listed opposite are those believed to have been worn and where there is evidence of markedly different colours, these are given in brackets. In the case of the *pouffes*, the uppermost colour is given first.

The Cavalry

Included in the Army of the Orient were two regiments of light cavalry – the 2nd/7th (*7me bis*) *Hussars* and the 22me Chasseurs à Cheval; and the 3rd, 14th, 15th, 18th and 20th Regiments of Dragoons. There was no heavy cavalry. The tasks of the light cavalry were reconnaissance, screening and pursuit, while the dragoons provided mounted and dismounted support for the infantry. The establishment of a cavalry regiment varied from between three and six squadrons, of two companies each, a company supposedly containing 116 men. However, as the cavalry disembarked in Egypt only

Unit	Helmet Pouffe (From Sept. 1798)	Coat	Collar	Cuffs/Turnbacks	Piping
		←	(From October 1799)		→
Light DBs					
2nd	Green	Light Green	Dark Blue	Dark Blue	White
4th	White/Green	Light Green	Dark Brown (Crimson)	Dark Brown (Crimson)	White
21st	Yellow/Green	Sky Blue	Yellow	Yellow (Red turnbacks)	White
22nd	Red/Green	Sky Blue	Maroon	Maroon	White
Line DBs					
9th	Red	Red	Green (Blue)	Green (White)	Green (Red/White)
13th	Dark Blue	Brown/Purple (Crimson)	Blue	Dark Brown (Puce)	White (Green)
18th	Black	Red (Brown)	Dark Brown (Scarlet) (Yellow)	Yellow (Blue)	Yellow (Blue or White)
25th	White/Red	Dusty Pink	Pale Blue	Pale Blue	White
32nd	White/Blue	Dusty Pink (Brown)	Dark Blue (Red)	Dark Blue (Orange)	White (Black or Blue)
61st	White/Black	Dark Brown (Crimson)	Dark Yellow (Blue)	Dark Yellow (Blue or Green)	Yellow (White)
69th	White/Yellow	Brown	Red	Red	White (Black or Blue)
75th	Red/Dark Blue	Red	Sky Blue	Sky Blue	White (Blue)
85th	Red/Yellow	Dark Brown	Red, piped Blue	Pale Yellow	White (Black or Blue)
88th	Blue/Yellow	Violet (Crimson)	Dark Blue (White bastion loop)	Green (Dark Blue)	White

totalled 2,700, the average regimental strength was just under 400 sabres.

The force also included 180 *Guides à Cheval* for duties around the headquarters and, from 9 January 1799, a *Régiment des Dromedaires* of two squadrons, each containing four companies of three officers, a trumpeter and 59 men. The latter was a unit of mounted infantry, which fought on foot to protect the French columns against swiftly-moving bands of Arab horsemen, using their camels for rapid deployment.

For the initial operations all seven cavalry regiments were grouped in one division. Detachments from each regiment except the 3rd Dragoons, totalling about 1,000 sabres, joined Desaix's operations in Upper Egypt, and for the campaign in Syria a smaller cavalry division of 800 sabres was formed under Murat, consisting of one squadron each of the Hussars, Chasseurs and 20th Dragoons and the 13th, 14th and 18th Dragoons complete, less detachments with Desaix. All regiments were present at the Battle of Alexandria in 1801, together with 130 'Dromedaries', but each regiment only averaged 160 sabres.

Although all hussars wore the dolman, pelisse and the mirliton felt cap with a '*flamme*', the colour of the clothing varied between regiments. There is some conflict of evidence as to whether, in 1798, the 2nd/7th wore the green dolman and pelisse with red facings and breeches of the 7th Hussars or a scarlet dolman with blue pelisse and breeches; however, after the infantry received its multi-coloured

Battle of Alexandria. To the right sits the wounded Abercromby surrounded by his staff. On his right are a soldier of the Minorca Regiment with a captured colour, and a sergeant of the 42nd Highlanders, pointing towards a gunner, Royal Artillery. Stuart's Foreign Brigade advances on the left. Engraving after the painting by P. J. de Loutherbourg. (National Army Museum)

uniforms in October 1799, the 2nd/7th had a dark blue dolman and breeches with scarlet facings and pelisse. From 24 September of the same year, their mirlitons, which probably had a scarlet '*flamme*', were fitted with peaks.

At the time of the Egyptian campaign, the uniform of the Chasseurs was undergoing a period of transition, gradually losing the crested leather helmet and cut-away *habit-dolman* of the 1792–95 period, and assuming the style of the hussars – though retaining its all-green colour with different regimental facings, which for the 22nd were dark orange. Around 1795 the helmet gave way to the mirliton, to which some regiments fixed a peak, and this in turn was transformed, by about 1800, into a '*shako à flamme*'. When these changes affected the 22nd cannot be stated with certainty, but according to the regulations of October 1799 the regiment was to have a light green dolman, and an apple green pelisse, with facings of its '*couleur distinctive capucine*' (nasturtium).

The Dragoons had brass helmets with brown fur turbans and black horse-hair crests, long green *habits* cut like the infantry's with regimental facings, white waistcoats, buff breeches and long boots. The facing colours were allotted to regiments in groups of six, individual regiments being distinguished by which parts of the coat bore the facing colour. Thus the 14th, 15th and 18th Dragoons all had facings of pink rose, which appeared on the lapels, turnbacks and cuff flaps of all three, but only on the cuffs of the 14th and the collars of the 15th and 18th, the collar of the former and the cuffs of the two latter being green. The 15th and 18th were distinguished by having horizontal and vertical pocket flaps respectively. The 3rd had all these items scarlet except for green cuffs, while the 20th had yellow lapels, turnbacks and cuffs; both had horizontal pockets. Throughout the dress changes of the campaign the Dragoons kept their green *habits* and helmets, but from 19th June 1799 they adopted hussar boots.

The *Guides à Cheval* wore a hat with a red-over-green plume, a green *surtout* faced red, red waistcoat laced yellow, yellow breeches and hussar boots, a costume which subsequently formed the basis for that of the *Chasseurs à Cheval* of the Imperial Guard. The dress of the 'Dromedaries' underwent several changes of detail but was essentially an hussar uniform in sky-blue without pelisse but with, in full dress, a scarlet caftan. The headgear was, consecutively, a turban, a turbanned shako or '*cahouq*', and finally, from October 1800, a black shako, while the bicorne was worn in undress.

Hussars, Chasseurs and Guides were armed with

a carbine of the 1786 model, two pistols and a sabre. Corporals and troopers of Dragoons had a short musket of the 1777 model, a bayonet, pistol and a long sword, while NCOs of the rank of sergeant and above and trumpeters had a sabre and two pistols. At first the 'Dromedaries' had a sabre, pistols and a lance but the latter was replaced by a musket with bayonet permanently attached to it by cords. The light cavalry accoutrements consisted of a pouch belt, with carbine swivel attached, and a waistbelt with sword slings from which, in the case of Hussars, a sabretache was suspended. Dragoons wore a sling waistbelt with bayonet frog under their coats and a pouch belt without firearm attachment, their muskets being secured by means of a bucket to the saddlery. The 'Dromedaries' had a sling waistbelt for the sabre and an infantry pouch belt.

Artillery and Engineers

A regulation of 7 May 1795 organised the Artillery into eight Foot regiments, each of 20 companies; eight Horse, each of six companies; twelve companies of *Ouvriers* and a battalion of Pontooneers. An artillery company usually had six cannon and two howitzers. A Foot company, so-called because all its gunners marched, consisted of five officers and 88 men, while a Horse company, in which the gunners either rode or were mounted on the limbers, had five officers and 72 men, although few of the companies in Egypt were up to strength.

Embarked for Egypt were four Horse companies plus detachments and fourteen of Foot, most of the latter from the 4th Regiment; in addition each infantry division had its own artillery company. This force of gunners manned 35 siege guns, mainly 24-pounders; 72 field guns, amongst which 12- and 8-pounders predominated; 24 howitzers and 40 mortars.

The cannon fired two main types of ammunition: round shot, which from a 12-pounder had an effective range of 900 metres, increasing to a maximum range of 1,800 metres, and from an 8-pounder between 800 and 1,500 metres; and canister, with effective ranges of 600 and 500 metres respectively. Canister could also be fired from howitzers, though with an effective range of only 200 metres; the chief howitzer projectiles were explosive shells, the range of which, from a 6-inch howitzer, varied between 700 and 1,200 metres, depending on the charge and fuse settings. The average rate of fire varied from one round per minute for a 12-pounder or 6-inch howitzer, to two per minute for an 8-pounder, while the lighter 4- or 6-pounders used by horse companies could get off up to three per minute.

For engineering tasks the Army of the Orient included 38 Engineer officers and companies of

Camp of the 61st Foot during the desert advance of Baird's contingent. Water colour by Private Porter, 61st Foot. (**National Army Museum**)

Above:
Fusilier, Demi-Brigade de Ligne. (Brunon Collection, National Army Museum photo)
Centre:
Officer, 4me Demi-Brigade Légère, in the 1799 clothing. Water colour by H. Boisselier. (Anna S. K. Brown Military Collection, Providence, Rhode Island)
Right:
Officer, 9me Demi-Brigade de Ligne, in the 1799 clothing. Water colour by H. Boisselier. (Anna S. K. Brown Military Collection, Providence, Rhode Island)

Sappers and Miners totalling a further 38 officers and 1,101 men, some companies being attached to divisions with the rest centralised as headquarters troops. The Army also had a company of balloonists (*aërostiers*) but since their balloon was destroyed during the Battle of the Nile, no tactical use could be made of it during the campaign.

The uniform of the Artillery was all dark blue with red cuffs, turnbacks and piping; the dress and accoutrements of the Horse followed that of the hussars but without the pelisse, while the Foot's was the same style as the infantry's, wearing bicornes like the grenadiers. When the infantry were put into cotton clothing in 1798, the artillery, like the cavalry, retained their cloth dress and continued to do so until the end of the campaign in 1801, although the 1799 regulations made no provision for red cuffs on the Foot's coats. The dress of the Engineers resembled that of the Foot Artillery but with black collars, cuffs and lapels, the men having red epaulettes. After October 1799 the Sappers and Miners had all-blue coats, the former with red collars and piping and the latter black collars and cuffs, though whether these coats retained the earlier cut or followed the pattern of the short infantry jackets is uncertain.

Fighting Capacity of the Army of the Orient
On landing in Egypt its fighting strength was:

INFANTRY: Five divisions (4 Light Demi-Brigades, 10 Line, Légion Malte)	28,000
CAVALRY: One division (7 regiments)	2,700
ARTILLERY AND ENGINEERS (131 guns, 40 mortars)	3,000
GUIDES (Horse and Foot)	480
Total	34,180

By 1801, when the British landed, the total strength, according to French sources, was 25,000; moderate British estimates put it at 27,000. The strongest demi-brigade in 1798, the 13th, could only muster 840 at the Battle of Alexandria, while the 61st could only field 500 bayonets. The only increases in strength had been from men enlisted in Egypt, and the arrival of a 200-strong detachment of the 51st Line and an artillery company in March 1801.

Although most of the troops were seasoned veterans of Bonaparte's victorious Army of Italy, they had never been well-disciplined and, after a long sea voyage, they were so appalled by the heat, the thirst and the savagery of the Mamelukes that the officers proved insubordinate and the men's morale sank. Nevertheless, cajoled and coerced by Bonaparte, they fought stoutly at the Battle of the Pyramids and the victory raised their spirits. However, once they reached Cairo, disease, homesickness and the knowledge that they were cut off by Nelson's victory at the Nile caused a further deterioration. Spirits rose with the invasion of Syria but fell once again due to sickness, the failure to take Acre and the hardships of the withdrawal back to Egypt. As Fortescue wrote: 'Though Bonaparte had compelled them to obedience, he had failed to constrain them to content'. Only in Desaix's division, despite its arduous campaign in Upper Egypt, does morale seem to have remained consistently good. The cheering effects of Bonaparte's crushing defeat of the Turks at Aboukir in July 1799 were almost immediately confounded by his abandonment of the army a month later. His successor, Kléber, worked hard and fruitfully to restore the troops' morale and his attempts to make peace raised their hopes for a safe return to France but, following his assassination, the incompetence and unpopularity of the next commander, Menou, made the army feel increasingly abandoned.

Drummer, Sapper, Grenadier, and Fusilier of 88me Demi-Brigade de Ligne; a contemporary drawing. (Gazette des Uniformes/National Army Museum photo)

Soldier, 14me Régiment de Dragons; a contemporary water colour. (Brunon Collection/National Army Museum photo)

Despite this, the British landing put them on their mettle once more and at Alexandria they displayed all their old dash and spirit. Though finally defeated and forced to surrender, the sense of failure was mitigated by the imminent departure for France, and this greatly tried army left Egypt with relief.

Tactics

The tactical doctrine of the Revolutionary Army was governed by the 1791 Drill Book which favoured a combination of line and column, depending on the task in hand, the terrain, and the enemy capabilities. However, manoeuvres of any sophistication proved to be beyond the largely untrained conscript levies, who had to be grouped into dense masses, covered by swarms of skirmishers, which then bludgeoned their way through the formal arrays of their opponents, who had previously been weakened by the fire of the artillery and the skirmishers. These crude tactics enjoyed surprising success but were expensive in casualties, and the undisciplined enthusiasm of the massed

Gunner, Artillerie à Cheval, 1798; lithograph after Adam. (National Army Museum)

columns could turn rapidly into panic-stricken flight if really determined opposition was met.

As the conscripts acquired more experience, it became possible to harness the shock value of the mass attack to an increased fire effect, provided by more controlled tactical formations. This was best seen in the combination of line and column, known as '*l'ordre mixte*', which had been used in the Italian campaign of 1796–97 and was therefore well-known to the Army of the Orient. Applied to a demi-brigade, this had the centre battalion formed in line three-deep to produce fire, with shock action provided by the other two on either flank in double-company columns, i.e. with two companies, each in three ranks, side by side in line forming a 'division', the other 'divisions' similarly arrayed one behind the other. The front of the whole formation was covered by a company from each battalion deployed as skirmishers. In this formation, discounting the skirmishers, the battalions in column, if at full strength, would have a frontage of 80 men each and a depth of twelve ranks, with a yard between ranks and three between 'divisions', while the battalion in line would be 320 men wide and three ranks deep. When in '*l'ordre mixte*', it was a simple manoeuvre for the centre battalion to form column, thus producing three battalion columns giving an attack formation with depth, or for the flank

battalions to deploy into line to provide maximum fire effect, or, if attacked by cavalry, for all three battalions to form squares.

As the opponents first encountered by the Army of the Orient bore no resemblance to those met in Europe, different measures were necessary, as will be seen later; against the British in 1801 the Army employed its well-tested European tactics but encountered for the first time a disciplined musketry with which they would become increasingly and depressingly familiar over the next fourteen years.

The Mameluke and Turkish Armies

Although later in the 19th Century the forces of the Ottoman Empire were to be re-organised on European lines, the armies against which the French found themselves opposed in Egypt and Syria, and with which the British would be allied in 1801, were little more than an oriental horde. Superbly mounted, plentifully if somewhat archaically armed, they were formidable in their way but bore little resemblance to an organised, disciplined European force of all arms, and their tactics, particularly those of the horse, had changed little over the centuries.

The chief threat with which the French had to contend was the Mameluke cavalry. The Mamelukes had first appeared in Egypt in the 13th Century, when the then-Sultan had imported some 1,200 youths of Georgian and Circassian stock from the Caucasus to form an élite body of troops. Since that time and even after the Turkish conquest of Egypt in 1517, the Mamelukes, while paying lip service to the nominal authority of the Turkish governor appointed by Constantinople, had dominated the country. Replenishing their numbers not from the indigenous population or even by natural reproduction amongst their own kind, but by importing fresh supplies of boys from the Caucasus, they created and maintained a superior warrior caste which exercised absolute power over the native inhabitants.

Each Mameluke was mounted on an Arab stallion and had a number of foot servants-at-arms who provided a sort of infantry. When charging at full gallop, the Mameluke would discharge his carbine, fire his several pairs of pistols, fling his javelins, and finally throw himself on his enemy scimitar in hand – sometimes with one in either hand – while holding his reins between his teeth. Brilliantly attired in turbans and layers of vests and caftans, utterly fearless, trained in equitation and skill-at-arms since childhood, they were excellent light cavalry material, yet knew no manoeuvres other than the headlong charge or, if repulsed, equally rapid flight. The role of their servants-at-arms was simply to mop up after the charge, finish off any survivors and retrieve the firearms discarded by their masters during their onslaught.

In Egypt, besides the Mameluke cavalry which numbered at best 9,000–10,000 and their 20,000-odd foot servants, there were various types of local forces nominally under the Turkish governor's authority, such as mounted Mustapharagas and Spahis and Janissary infantry, totalling some 20,000. In addition there were bands of mounted Bedouin Arabs from the desert tribes, whose only use was for harassing attacks against stragglers and supply columns; and mobs of impressed *fellahin* armed with little more than clubs.

Among the main Turkish forces in Syria the renowned Janissary infantry with their white bonnets were similar in some respects to the Mamelukes, forming an élite corps, recruited originally from boys taken from the Balkan provinces of the Ottoman Empire, converted to Islam and rigorously trained in arms. Once the terror of Europe, by the beginning of the 19th Century they were in decline as a fighting force, having become arrogant, insubordinate and a law unto themselves. They were grouped into 'Ortahs', of which there were about 150; but the numbers in each varied enormously, according to its re-putation, a famous one having as many as 30,000. In 1800 there were perhaps 400,000 Janissaries in the Ottoman Empire. Each man provided his own weapons, usually a musket and one or more side-arms. Apart from the Janissaries, a Turkish army was raised on feudal lines, the *pasha* of each territory being required to assemble a given number of followers, armed and accoutred at his expense.

The most stalwart and reliable of the Turkish troops in the Egyptian campaigns were the Al-banian and Moroccan infantry, such as defied Bonaparte at the siege of El Arish. When well-led and properly organised, as the Turkish garrison of Acre was by Sir Sydney Smith and the French emigré artillery officer, Colonel Phélipeaux, the Turkish soldier proved that he was good fighting material, as General John Moore reported when sent to evaluate the efficiency of the Turkish army in early 1801. However, under the existing Turkish administration, Moore considered the army to be 'a wild, ungovernable mob', from which it was 'vain to expect any co-operation'.

The British Army

In the late 18th Century the ranks of the British Army were recruited by voluntary enlistment from the most deprived, though not necessarily criminal, sections of society while its officers were drawn from the aristocracy and the gentry, who acquired their commissions and most of their promotion by purchase, and knowledge of their profession by

Soldier of the Régiment de Dromedaires in undress uniform, 1801; a contemporary engraving. (National Army Museum)

Officer and gunner, Artillerie à Pied, 1797; a contemporary water colour. (Anna S. K. Brown Military Collection, Providence, Rhode Island)

experience. Although the performance of the Army in the American War of Independence had been more creditable than its ultimate defeat would suggest, its efficiency had since declined and the campaigns in the Low Countries, which followed the outbreak of the French Revolutionary War, revealed that it was in no condition to undertake a major European conflict. It was not an integrated force at all, rather a collection of largely autonomous and under-strength regiments of horse and foot, with no brigade or divisional organisation, no staff system and a dire lack of logistical support. The methods of recruitment, commissioning and supply all invited peculation, and the regiments were widely dispersed, often condemned to endure unhealthy stations for long periods.

Yet, by the turn of the century, there were signs of hope. The Duke of York, though a failure as a field commander in Flanders, was displaying skill and foresight as a reforming administrator; the overall strength had increased by 40% since 1795; several very able officers were coming to the fore, and new tactical ideas were being generated. Regimental officers, if professionally unskilled, were usually courageous and self-confident, while the soldiers, sternly disciplined, constantly drilled in manoeuvre and musketry, indoctrinated in the spirit of their regiments and fortified by their own grim humour, could be relied upon for steadfast endurance. Though lacking the élan and individuality of the French conscript, the redcoat seldom displayed the former's volatility. It was in fact an Army on the brink of one of its most splendid epochs.

The Infantry

In 1800 the Infantry consisted of three regiments of Foot Guards and 94 of the Line. The tactical unit was not the regiment but the battalion, of which the 1st Guards had three, the Coldstream and 3rd Guards two each, while the Line regiments, with the exception of the 1st and 60th Foot, normally had only one. However, the war with France had

Soldier, 22me Chasseurs à Cheval; a water colour by H. Boisselier. (Anna S. K. Brown Military Collection, Providence, Rhode Island)

required 16 regiments to raise second and, in some cases, third battalions, drawn from the Militia for limited service in Europe only. These, together with the two battalions always enjoyed by the 1st Foot and the six of the 60th, who were mainly foreigners, gave the Line a total of 118 battalions.

The Line regiments were numbered consecutively, most having a subsidiary royal or territorial title; three were designated Fusiliers, though unlike the French service this title had no functional significance, and eleven were Highlanders. The tactics of the French armies in the Low Countries had highlighted the dearth of light troops in the British infantry and the 90th Foot, raised in 1794 as a personal contribution to the war by a Scottish gentleman, Thomas Graham of Balgowan,

Mamelukes and Bedouin Arab; an engraving from Walsh's *Journal of the Campaign in Egypt* (1803). (National Army Museum)

Turkish infantry and cavalry, from Walsh's *Journal of the Campaign in Egypt* (1803). (National Army Museum)

was equipped and trained as a light infantry corps. The deficiency was further recognised by the formation, in 1797, of a green-jacketed battalion of the 60th armed with rifles and, in 1800, by an Experimental Corps of Riflemen (later the 95th).

An infantry battalion at full war establishment numbered just under 1,200 officers and men and was organised into ten companies. The best soldiers were drawn off for the two flank companies, the tallest and strongest forming the grenadiers, the best marksmen and the most nimble the light infantry company. A company at full strength

contained four officers, five sergeants, two drummers, five corporals and 95 privates.

In 1800 the dress of the infantry lost most of its 18th Century appearance and acquired characteristics that would last, with various modifications, until well into the 19th Century. Although grenadiers, drummers and fusiliers retained their bearskin caps, the hats of the battalion men were replaced by a cylindrical leather shako, with a brass plate in front and a short plume – white-over-red for the battalion companies, green for the light infantry and white for the grenadiers, when they wore shakos. The red coat, with collar, cuffs and shoulder straps in each regiment's facing colour, now buttoned down to the waist and had short tails at the rear; the practice of embellishing the coat with regimental 'lace' continued, sergeants having plain white. White breeches and black gaiters up to the knee completed the costume, although white trousers for undress wear were also coming into favour. Officers still wore the cocked hat, which in Egypt was usually superseded by a round hat similar to a civilian's top hat, while their scarlet coats were double-breasted with long tails (except for Highland officers, whose coat-tails were short), and gold or silver buttons, lace and epaulettes according to regiment. Highlanders' coats were the same as the rest of the Line, being worn with kilt, diced hose and the blue bonnet, adorned with black ostrich feathers, which varied in number and size

British troops, left to right: Infantry Sergeant; Grenadier, Coldstream Guards; Gunner, Royal Artillery; Infantry Private. From De Bosset's Uniform Chart 1803. (National Army Museum)

where shock action was the province of the heavies and outpost duties that of the light cavalry, in the British service the distinction, apart from dress differences, was largely one of size and weight of man and horse, since both branches were expected to undertake all cavalry work. Furthermore, the heavy cavalry was only suitable for European service owing to the difficulty of obtaining large enough horses outside Europe. Hence the expeditionary force for Egypt included only Light Dragoons.

At the war establishment a cavalry regiment usually had five squadrons, each of two troops, although one or two of these squadrons would be left at home to recruit and train reinforcements. The administrative unit was the troop which at full strength had three officers, a troop-sergeant-major, three sergeants, four corporals, a trumpeter, a farrier and 63 privates.

Light Dragoons wore the black-crested helmet known as the 'Tarleton', a single-breasted, waist-length jacket in dark blue braided in the hussar style, white breeches and knee-length boots. The helmet had a white-over-red feather on the left side, a turban in the regimental facing colour, and a regimental device in white metal on the right. The collar and cuffs were in the facing colour, regiments with buff facings also having breeches and accoutrements in the same colour. Officers were dressed similarly to the men but with silver braid instead of white. Regiments serving in tropical stations, like the 8th Light Dragoons which sent a detachment to Egypt from the Cape, had light-grey jackets and a tin cap lined with white linen, which, in the 8th, was fitted with a brass crest, red horse-hair mane and turban.

The dragoon was armed with sabre, pistol and carbine. Whether the latter used by regiments in Egypt was the Paget carbine (16-inch barrel), introduced around 1800, or the earlier 1796 type (26-inch barrel) is uncertain. His accoutrements consisted of a pouch belt fitted with a carbine swivel and a sword belt with slings. As late as 1795 the latter was worn over the right shoulder but drawings made by Hamilton Smith in about 1800 show a much narrower waistbelt in use. In the mid-1790s dragoons were also armed with a bayonet, suspended in a frog from the sword belt, and although the 7th Light Dragoons were still pro-

between regiments. De Loutherbourg's paintings of the campaign show round hats only worn by officers, the men being in shakos, as would be expected, since Abercromby's force came entirely from Europe. However, in the 61st Foot, which came up from the Cape to join Baird's Indian contingent, all ranks had round hats, as was probably the case with the British regiments from India.

The infantryman was armed with either the Brown Bess musket (Short Land Pattern) with 42-inch barrel or the India Pattern (39-inch barrel), both taking the 17-inch socket bayonet. Light company sergeants had a shorter firearm, while other sergeants carried a 9-foot pike. Battalion officers and sergeants had a straight sword of the 1796 pattern, flank company officers a sabre, and Highland officers and sergeants a broadsword. The soldier was accoutred with pouch and bayonet belts, which were secured on the chest by a belt plate of regimental pattern, and a painted canvas knapsack. When proceeding on active service, items classified as camp equipage, such as haversacks, water bottles, blankets, billhooks, entrenching tools and cooking pots, were also issued.

The Cavalry

Apart from the Household Cavalry, there were, in 1800, twelve regiments of heavy cavalry and 29 of Light Dragoons. Unlike most continental armies vided with them in 1802, it is uncertain when they ceased to be part of the light dragoon's armament, perhaps with the introduction of the Paget carbine.

Artillery and Engineers

In 1800 the artillery and engineers were quite separate from the rest of the Army, being controlled, not by the Horse Guards, but by the Board of Ordnance. Their officers were of a different calibre, their commissioning and promotion depending upon merit and seniority, not on purchase; and the men, particularly the gunners, were noted for their fine appearance and strength. The Royal Artillery included the Horse branch of eight troops and the Foot of six battalions, each of ten companies, each of five officers and 120 NCOs and men. The engineers also had two branches but of a different nature: the Royal Engineers, an all-officer corps, and the Royal Military Artificers, which contained a number of companies permanently stationed in various fortresses and garrisons, with officers supplied by the Royal Engineers. When engineers were required for an expedition such as Egypt, detachments were drawn from the different companies.

No horse artillery accompanied Abercromby's force but the Foot Artillery was represented by two companies of the 1st Battalion, three of the 5th, three detachments of the 2nd and one of the 4th. The guns in most common use were the light and medium 6-pounder and the 5½-inch howitzer, five of the former and one howitzer forming a battery (or brigade) manned by a company of gunners. There were also some 12- and 24-pounders as siege artillery. After the landing, the lack of horse artillery was badly felt and two detachments were formed from the foot companies to act with cavalry: one with four light 3-pounders brought from Malta and the other with four light 6-pounders and two howitzers, the gunners being mounted on the limbers and draught horses.

The 6-pounder had an effective range of between 750 and 1,200 metres with ball and 400 with canister, while the performance of the 5½-inch howitzer was roughly comparable with that of the French 6-inch weapon. In addition to the three types of projectile used by the French, British gunners also had shrapnel, a shell filled with iron balls and detonated by a pre-set fuse.

Apart from the foot batteries, it had long been the practice to attach two 6-pounders to each infantry battalion. Since 1795 these had ceased to be manned by the Royal Artillery and each battalion had to train one officer and 34 men in their use.

The dress of the Foot Artillery was largely the same as the infantry but with blue coats faced red, the men's having bastion-shaped loops of yellow lace. The uniform of the Royal Engineers and the Artificers approximated to that of the Artillery but with black facings, although the Artificers may not have received the shako, to replace the hat, until 1802. They also had a working dress of a blue cloth jacket with skirts, a serge waistcoat with sleeves, blue serge pantaloons, black half-gaiters and a round hat.

Artillery and engineer officers had the 1796 infantry sword, while artillerymen and artificers also had infantry weapons and accoutrements. The pouch worn by the Foot Artillery was of white leather and to its belt were secured a priming flask, two vent-prickers and a hammer. These fittings did not permit the wearing of a belt plate, nor was one worn by the artificers, who had a large brass buckle instead.

British infantry shako, 1800 pattern; note the folding flap at the rear. (National Army Museum)

Officer, 7th Royal Fusiliers, 1800. Fusilier regiments were represented in Egypt by the 23rd Royal Welch, whose uniform was very similar. (British Military Library, via National Army Museum)

Foreign Regiments

The grave shortage of troops on the outbreak of the French Revolutionary War persuaded the Government to sanction the raising of foreign regiments for inclusion in the British Army. The 60th Foot had always been a predominantly foreign corps but, between 1793 and 1802, nearly 80 foreign units of horse, foot and artillery were raised by French royalists, British officers, German princelings and sundry adventurers from men of many nationalities whose lives, in one way or another, had been upset by the Revolution. Some units had a very short life and all varied greatly in quality, from excellent regiments like the Loyal Emigrants, many of whose soldiers were ex-officers of the French Royal Army, to others that were little more than gangs of deserters and criminals.

The story of these regiments and the variety of their uniforms is a fascinating study in itself but here it is only possible to notice those that fought in Egypt. The Corsican Rangers, formed as a light infantry corps in Minorca in 1799 from Corsicans who had fled their native island, fought with John Moore's Reserve and were sufficiently well-trained and disciplined to be entrusted with outpost duties. They were dressed in green with black facings and accoutrements and wore the British shako, officers having round hats. John Stuart's Foreign Brigade included three regiments: de Roll's, formed mainly from ex-soldiers of the Swiss Guards of the Bourbons in 1794; Dillon's, formed in 1795 from French émigrés and some Italians; and the Minorca Regiment, formed in 1799 from German and Swiss prisoners of war taken in Minorca. The first two had deteriorated in 1797 but by 1800 had been brought to perfect discipline by General Charles Stuart, under whose command they came in the Mediterranean and who had formed the Minorca Regiment. All three performed well in Egypt. Each was dressed and accoutred like British infantry, Dillon's and the Minorca having yellow facings, de Roll's sky-blue. Officers of the Minorca wore a round hat with a black fur crest and there is evidence that the soldiers of de Roll's all wore round hats and white gaiter-trousers.

In the Cavalry Brigade was a detachment of Hompesch's Mounted Rifles. Baron Charles de Hompesch, a Prussian hussar colonel, and his brother Ferdinand raised a number of units for British service, among which was a corps of light troops, some of them mounted. The dismounted element passed into the 60th and the Mounted Rifles were established as a separate corps in 1798, its men being mostly Germans with some French émigrés among the officers. They acquired an excellent reputation in the Irish Rebellion of 1798, which they fully maintained in Egypt until three vedettes deserted, an offence for which the whole detachment was deprived of its horses and put into garrison at Aboukir. The uniform was green, faced red, with red breeches and red shako.

Among the reinforcements sent to Egypt in mid-1801 was a second foreign brigade: de Watteville's

Regiment, formed in 1801 from Swiss troops who had been fighting alongside the Austrians; Löwenstein's Jägers, raised in Bavaria by Prince Löwenstein-Wertheim from Poles, Germans, Walloons and French émigrés; and the *Chasseurs Britanniques*, formed in 1801 from the remains of the émigré Army of Condé, the men being chiefly Germans, Swiss and Poles. The last two were both light infantry corps. De Watteville's always enjoyed an excellent reputation, and Löwenstein's performed efficiently in Egypt but the *Chasseurs* were always prone to disciplinary troubles. In Egypt none of these regiments had British style uniforms: de Watteville's wore green jackets faced black with bright blue pantaloons and half-gaiters, Löwenstein's grey-blue jackets and pantaloons with half-gaiters and green facings, and the *Chasseurs* green jackets faced black or yellow, grey pantaloons and half-gaiters. The two latter both had black accoutrements and British headgear, Löwenstein's wearing round hats and the *Chasseurs* the infantry shako with bugle-horn badge. De

Watteville's wore the shako of the Swiss regiment of Rovéréa which was cylindrical, with a flat peak and a black turban around it.

Finally, but in an entirely different category from these foreign regiments, were the three battalions of Sepoys from the Honourable East India Company's forces, which formed part of Baird's contingent: the 2nd/1st and 1st/7th Bombay Native Infantry and a composite battalion of Bengal Native Infantry. These were organised, armed and equipped similarly to British infantry and although there were differences in uniform between the Bombay and Bengal armies, in general the Sepoy wore a curious turban headdress, stiffened to resemble a low bell-topped shako, a short cut-away red coat with collar, cuffs and lapels in the facing colour, and white drawers, the legs being left bare.

Group of officers around the wounded Abercromby at Alexandria. Note on the right Colonel Stirling in the uniform of the 42nd Highlanders. Engraving after Stothard. (National Army Museum)

Fighting Capacity of Abercromby's Army

The strength returns for the force just before it sailed from Turkey for Egypt give the following figures of fit men, excluding officers:

INFANTRY: 3 brigades of 4 battalions,
    2 of 3, 1 of 2, Reserve of 5   14,555
CAVALRY: 2 regiments, 2 detachments   1,125
ARTILLERY   667
Total   16,347

In addition there were just over 1,000 men sick but present with the force, so that, with officers included, Abercromby had a strength of around 17,000, roughly two-thirds of Menou's army. Before the Battle of Alexandria he was reinforced by the 2nd/27th Foot and a battalion of Marines. Between May–July a further seven British and three foreign battalions were landed, plus the 22nd Light Dragoons.

Baird's Indian contingent of four British and three Indian battalions landed in the Red Sea in May–June where it was joined by the detachment of 8th Light Dragoons and the 61st Foot from the Cape, but although this force endured some very hard marching, it was not engaged against the main French army.

After its defeats in the Low Countries and wasteful operations in the West Indies, the British Army in 1800 was badly in need of success. Abercromby had been appointed to the Mediterranean command in April 1800 but, given a multitude of tasks by the Government which were quite beyond his resources, his operations were abortive. The decision to invade Egypt gave his troops their first worthwhile mission and, despite their relative weakness in strength and the hazardous nature of the undertaking, or perhaps because of it, their spirits rose to the occasion.

Abercromby himself was one of the most competent and best-loved senior officers in the service and, by careful preparation and training in Turkey, did all he could to ensure the operation's success. He was well-served by his subordinates. His deputy, Sir John Hely-Hutchinson, though lacking Abercromby's popularity, was to prove a capable successor after his death. His brigade commanders included Moore, already marked as a brilliant officer, Hope, Oakes and Craddock. There were battalion commanders such as Rowland Hill of the 90th, later Wellington's most trusted divisional and corps commander; and Edward Paget of the 28th who, though only 24, was considered an 'officer of great promise', and would later command the rearguard division during the retreat to Corunna. It was Paget who summed up the quality of Abercromby's troops thus: 'There is a certain devil in this army that will carry it through thick and thin. It is the first fair trial between Englishmen and Frenchmen during the whole of this war and at no former period of our history did John Bull ever hold his enemy cheaper'.

Tactics

The British service had long favoured the line as the most effective fighting formation and, while its experience in the Low Countries of the new French tactics had alerted the authorities to their own lack of light troops, their faith in the ability of rapid and accurate fire, as produced by the maximum number of muskets deployed in line, to counter the shock effect of bayonets in solid columns, remained unshaken. The current manual, Sir David Dundas' 'Principles of Military Movements', issued in 1792, required a three-deep line (a formation that had failed continental armies against the French); but by reverting to the earlier two-deep deployment, as was done in Egypt, not only could every man use his musket freely, but the frontage of the enemy columns, even in '*l'ordre mixte*', could always be overlapped. So faith was pinned on fire effect, soldiers were constantly practised in musketry, and

Soldier's ammunition pouch, 50th Foot. (National Army Museum)

France:
1 Dragoon, 3ᵐᵉ Régt. de Dragons, 1798
2 Général de Division, 1798
3 Grenadier, 18ᵐᵉ Demi-Brigade de Ligne, 1798

G. A. EMBLETON

A

France:
1 Carabinier, 21me Demi-Brigade Légère, 1798-99
2 Officer, 22me Régt. de Chasseurs à Cheval, 1798
3 Fusiliers, 75me Demi-Brigade de Ligne, 1798-99

B

G. A. EMBLETON

France:
1 Hussar, 7me bis Régt. de Hussards, 1799
2 Officer, 18me Régt. de Dragons, 1799
3 Chasseur, 22me Demi-Brigade Légère, 1798-99

France:
1 Drummer, 88me Demi-Brigade de Ligne, 1799-1801
2 Field Officer, 4me Demi-Brigade Légère, 1799-1801
3 Fusilier, 69me Demi-Brigade de Ligne, 1799-1801

D

G. A. EMBLETON

Britain:
1 Major-General, 1801
2 Private, Light Coy., 28th Foot, 1801
3 Major, Corsican Rangers, 1801

Britain:
1 Private, 12th Light Dragoons, 1801
2 Officer, Grenadier Coy., 58th Foot, 1801
3 Drummer, 40th Foot, 1801

F

Britain:
1 Private, 90th Foot, 1801
2 Sergeant, battalion coy., 3rd Foot Guards, 1801
3 Private, Hompesch's Mounted Rifles, 1801

G. A. EMBLETON

G

Britain:

1 Gunner, Royal Artillery, 1801
2 Sergeant-Major, 92nd Foot, 1801
3 Private, battalion coy., de Watteville's Swiss Regt., 1801

H

G. A. EMBLETON

the infantry deployed with each company and battalion in two ranks beside the other. To counter the enemy skirmishers, the battalion light companies were advanced in front, and these, as has been seen, were being augmented by the formation of light regiments, British and foreign. Column, of companies, half-companies or sections, was reserved for manoeuvre, it being a simple matter to form line from this formation.

The line, if its flanks were unprotected, was vulnerable to cavalry, which would normally be received in battalion squares. However in Egypt, despite several charges on infantry by French cavalry, there is no record of squares being formed. The 90th Foot routed one charge from an L-shaped formation; the 28th in the famous incident at Alexandria simply turned the rear rank about; while the Minorca Regiment, when charged in line, opened the line, fired as the cavalry poured through the gaps and repeated the process when the horsemen returned, inflicting heavy casualties. The line of the 42nd was broken by cavalry but each Highlander continued fighting on his own ground until the line could be reformed.

British cavalry charged in line and moved in column. In Egypt, much weaker than the French and short of horses, the small cavalry force, though full of dash, displayed little skill and in about the only horse-versus-horse encounter was severely bested. Although useful work was performed as flank guards during the advance on Cairo, its efficiency was well short of the infantry's.

Regimental Dress Distinctions, 1801

Regiment	Facings	Officers' Lace	Soldiers' White Lace Arrangement; Colour of Stripes
8 LD†	Red	Silver	White
11 LD	Buff	Silver	White
12 LD	Pale yellow	Silver	White
22 LD*	Red	Silver	White
26 LD	Blue	Silver	White
Hompesch's	Red	Gold	Nil
R.A.	Red	Gold	Bastion, regular; yellow lace
R.E. & Artificers	Black	Gold	Bastion, regular; yellow lace
Coldstream Gds	Blue	Gold	Pairs; plain
3rd Guards	Blue	Gold	Threes; plain
1st Foot	Blue	Gold	Pairs; double blue worm
2nd	Blue	Silver	Regular; blue
8th	Blue	Gold	Regular; blue & yellow
10th†	Bright yellow	Silver	Regular; blue
13th	Philemot yellow	Silver	Pairs; yellow
18th	Blue	Gold	Pairs; blue
20th*	Pale yellow	Silver	Pairs; red & black
23rd (Fusiliers)	Blue	Gold	Bastion, regular; red, blue & yellow
24th*	Willow green	Silver	Pairs; red & green
25th*	Deep yellow	Gold	Bastion, regular; blue, yellow & red
26th*	Pale yellow	Silver	Pairs; 1 blue, 2 yellow
27th	Buff	Gold	Regular; blue & red
28th	Bright yellow	Silver	Pairs; 1 yellow, 2 black
30th	Pale yellow	Silver	Bastion, regular; sky-blue
40th	Buff	Gold	Regular; red & black
42nd (Highlanders)	Blue	Gold	Bastion, regular; red
44th	Yellow	Silver	Regular; blue, yellow & black

Regiment	Facings	Officers' Lace	Soldiers' White Lace Arrangement; Colour of Stripes
50th	Black	Silver	Pairs; red
54th	Popinjay green	Silver	Pairs; green
58th	Black	Gold	Regular; red
61st†	Buff	Silver	Regular; blue
79th (Highlanders)	Dark green	Gold	Pairs; 1 yellow, 2 red
80th†	Yellow	Gold	Pairs; 2 red, 1 black
86th†	Yellow	Silver	Pairs; 2 yellow, 2 black
88th†	Pale yellow	Silver	Pairs; 2 black, 2 red, 1 yellow
89th	Black	Gold	Pairs; red & blue
90th	Deep buff	Gold	Pairs; blue & buff
92nd (Highlanders)	Yellow	Silver	Pairs; blue
Minorca	Yellow	Silver	Regular; black
De Roll's	Sky-blue	Silver	Regular; blue
Dillon's	Yellow	Silver	Bastion, regular; dark grey
Corsican Rangers	Black	Silver	White lace, collar & cuffs only; buttons regular
De Watteville's*	Black	Gold	No lace; buttons regular
Chasseurs Britanniques*	Black or yellow	Silver	No lace; half-lapels in black, 2 rows of buttons, regular
Löwenstein's*	Dark green	Unknown	No lace; half-lapels in dark green, 2 rows of buttons, regular
Bombay N.I.†	Yellow	Silver	Regular; plain
Bengal N.I.†	Blue or yellow	Unknown	Regular; plain
Ancient Irish Fencibles*	No details known		

Buttons Officers: Gilt or silver, according to lace.

Soldiers: All pewter or white metal, except:–

Royal Artillery & Artificers – bronze or brass.

De Watteville's & Löwenstein's – yellow metal.

† Baird's Contingent from India and the Cape.

* Reinforcing units, May–July 1801.

The Battles

After landing and capturing Alexandria in early July 1798, Bonaparte immediately advanced on Cairo. Following a few skirmishes with the Mamelukes, the first major battle occurred on the 21st within sight of the Pyramids, with Cairo only four miles away on the opposite bank of the Nile. The French were confronted, on the west bank, by Murad Bey with some 6,000 Mameluke cavalry and 12,000 *fellahin* infantry, while in and around Cairo itself was Ibrahim Bey with about 100,000 infantry. Realising that the Mameluke strength lay in the shock action of headlong cavalry charges, Bonaparte adopted a battle array of divisional

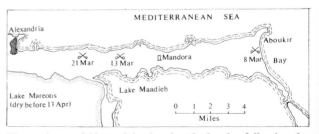

The environs of Alexandria showing the battles following the British landing in 1801.

squares, or rather rectangles, said to be his only tactical innovation. Each division had a complete demi-brigade, in six ranks, forming the front and rear faces of the rectangle, while the third was split up to form the two sides. All the cavalry and

Helmet, of Light Dragoon pattern, worn by the 90th Foot. The black bearskin crest is missing. This example was worn by Colonel Rowland Hill at the Battle of Mandora and was struck on the peak by a musket ball. (National Army Museum)

baggage were placed within the rectangles. The left division, under General Bon, rested on the Nile with the other four of Vial, Dugua, Reynier (where Bonaparte himself took post), and Desaix forming an oblique line to the south-west.

At 3.30 p.m. the Mameluke horse charged the French right, but despite their speed and courage they were unable to prevail against the massed musketry and artillery of Reynier and Desaix. While this chief threat was held on the right, Bon and Vial advanced to attack a fortified village on the Nile where, notwithstanding some heavy artillery fire, Bon formed some assaulting columns and, supported by three small squares, carried the village, cutting off the *fellahin's* retreat. After an hour's fighting the Mamelukes fled, having lost some 2,000 horsemen and several thousand *fellahin*, against French losses of 29 killed and about 200 wounded. Ibrahim's horde had been unable to influence the battle and, seeing Murad's defeat, drifted off into the desert.

Desaix's operations in Upper Egypt were a miracle of hard marching and well-fought actions in which, with no more than 3,000 men (21st, 61st and 88th Demi-Brigades) he managed to harrass and tie down a Mameluke force of more than three times his strength. While this was going on, the campaign of Syria proceeded, starting with the siege of El Arish, which held out for a surprising eleven days, and leading up to the protracted, eventually fruitless attempts to take Acre. During the latter, Kléber, with only 2,000 men, withstood assaults by 25,000 Turkish horse at Mount Tabor, using the same square formation as in the Pyramids battle, until Bonaparte could arrive with Bon's division to take the Turks in the rear.

Bonaparte's final battle, at Aboukir on 25 July 1799, saw a ferocious charge by the French cavalry under Murat which routed the Turks, whose entrenchments had previously been stormed by the French infantry.

Officer, 12th Light Dragoons, c.1800; a water colour by Robert Dighton. (Reproduced by gracious permission of Her Majesty The Queen)

Officer, Royal Artillery, 1799. In Egypt a round hat would have replaced the cocked hat shown here. Engraving from the British Military Library. (National Army Museum)

By March 1800, following the failure of Kléber's peace negotiations, 40,000 Turks were at the gates of Cairo. Kléber, with only a quarter of that strength, made a surprise dawn attack on them at Heliopolis. By nightfall he was victorious and within a week had driven them from Egypt.

To resist the British landing on 8 March 1801 the French deployed, among the sand-dunes of Abou-kir Bay, two-thirds of the 61st and 75th Demi-Brigades with elements of two others and about 180 Dragoons. The assault was made with dash under heavy fire by Moore's Reserve consisting of, on the right, the 23rd, 28th and 40th (four companies only) and on the left, the 42nd, 58th and Corsican Rangers, supported by the Guards and the 1st and 54th.

Following Moore's successful landing a sharp action was fought on 13th March at Mandora, where the 90th and 92nd, covering the advance of the army to Alexandria, resisted determined attacks by French cavalry and horse artillery until the rest of the force could deploy. After an inconclusive battle, Abercromby took up a defensive position four miles from Alexandria with his right on the Mediterranean shore and his left on the edge of the dried-up Lake Mareotis. Moore held the right with the 58th in some ruins on the shore, the 28th to their left front in a redoubt and his other battalions ready to support this vital flank. The position was prolonged to the left by the Guards, Coote's and Craddock's brigades, while Stuart's, Doyle's and Cavan's brigades, with the cavalry, formed a second line.

The battle of 21 March started just before dawn with a feint attack by Reynier's division (five demi-brigades) on the British left but, shortly after, the main assault by Lanusse's division (4th, 18th, 69th and 88th Demi-Brigades), supported by Rampon's (21st, 32nd, elements of 2nd and 25th) came in against the 28th and 58th Foot to turn the British right. Heavy fighting in semi-darkness ensued around the ruins and redoubt with the rest of the Reserve joining the struggle; but Moore's men held their ground, maintaining a continuous musketry from their double ranks against the French columns. Rampon then drew off his division to attack the Guards while Menou sent his cavalry to aid Lanusse against Moore, but the latter's battalions, supported by Stuart's foreign brigade, still could not be broken. With Rampon held at bay by the volleys from the Guards' line, the French attacks faded out and after continuing an artillery bombardment of the British positions for some time, Menou withdrew.

Although the French had been superior in numbers at the point of attack, the British held the advantage of the ground and, with their brigades deployed in line, demonstrated their superiority over the French columns. The latter's cavalry had displayed their usual spirit but could not prevail against disciplined musketry, while the British cavalry, many of whom were still without horses, hardly featured in the battle. The French left over a thousand dead on the field, the British suffering 243 killed, mostly from the Reserve. Abercromby and Lanusse both received mortal wounds and several brigadiers on both sides, including Moore, were wounded.

Menou now being bottled up in Alexandria,

Hutchinson left Coote with 6,000 men to contain him, sent part of the reserve with Hompesch's to capture Rosetta, and then advanced on Cairo, which he reached, after a few skirmishes, in mid-June. After receiving the surrender there and escorting the French garrison to the coast, he began the final reduction of Alexandria. Hutchinson now had 35 battalions. While the Reserve feinted to the east of the city, Coote with the Guards and two other brigades landed on 16 August to its west, where fierce opposition was met from Fort Marabout, which was eventually stormed by the 54th. Combined assaults were then mounted from both sides until 26 August when Menou asked for terms; on 14 September his troops embarked for France. The French adventure in Egypt, with its threat to India, was over and the British Army had enjoyed its first success of the Revolutionary War.

The Plates

(*NB* These notes should be read in conjunction with the paragraphs dealing with uniforms in the chapters on the respective armies.)

France:

A1 Dragoon, 3me Régiment de Dragons, 1798
The cuffs of this regiment were green, only the flaps being red, and the skirt pockets were set on horizontally with red piping. The shoulder belt had brass fittings and suspended a black leather pouch. The buff breeches and long boots were replaced, after 19 June 1799, by pantaloons and hussar boots. The bayonet scabbard can be seen suspended from the waistbelt and the fusil was secured to the saddlery. The plumes were not worn in action.

Field gun, Royal Artillery. Detail of an engraving after P. J. de Loutherbourg's *Battle of Maida, 1806.* **(National Army Museum)**

Anton Lutz, soldier of the Minorca Regiment, with the colour of the 21me Demi-Brigade Légère taken by him at the Battle of Alexandria. Engraving after Reinagle. (National Army Museum)

A2 Général de Division, 1798

This figure is based on portraits made in Egypt of Generals Kléber and Desaix. According to the work of Lienhart and Humbert, the grades of general officers – 'en chef', 'division' and 'brigade' – were chiefly distinguished by the arrangement of the tricoloured hat plumes and variations in the colour of the sashes, but from contemporary paintings it appears that senior officers exercised their own preferences and adorned themselves with a variety of plumes and sashes made up locally in Egypt. Mameluke sabres became popular with officers during the campaign.

A3 Grenadier, 18me Demi-Brigade de Ligne, 1798

This was the dress worn during the initial stages of the campaign. The hat could be worn 'en colonne', as here, or 'en bataille', i.e. athwart. The falling plume and red epaulettes were only worn by grenadiers, fusiliers having a flat, round, woollen pom-pom

coloured red with white centre, and blue shoulder straps piped red. The pocket flaps were set horizontally in the coat skirts and edged with red. The red-striped 'pantalons de route' were provided for this demi-brigade, the 25th, 32nd and 75th before sailing from Toulon. The forage cap is rolled beneath the ammunition pouch and a gourd for water is added to the normal accoutrements. The right shoulder belt suspends the sabre-briquet and bayonet; fusiliers simply had the bayonet attached to the pouch belt near the lower edge of the lapel.

B1 Carabinier, 21me Demi-Brigade Légère, 1798–99

This unit formed part of Desaix's division, which had left for Upper Egypt before the issue of cotton clothing and therefore had only their European uniforms, which were soon in rags. It seems inconceivable that the carabiniers would have worn their bearskin caps in the desert heat, though whether the chasseur companies wore hats with a

Battle of the Pyramids, 1798; an engraving after Swebach. (Anna S. K. Brown Military Collection, Providence, Rhode Island)

green plume or a shako, then becoming popular for the light infantry, is uncertain. Lejeune's painting of the Battle of the Pyramids shows bearskins and shakos worn by light infantrymen and the latter also appear in some drawings by Denon who accompanied the expedition. The epaulettes of *chasseurs* were all green except for a red crescent.

B2 Officer, 22me Régiment de Chasseurs à Cheval, 1798
Since, as stated earlier, the dress of these regiments was in a state of transition, there must be some uncertainty about this reconstruction. In Egypt the 22nd wore hats, rather than the mirliton or shako then being adopted by these regiments in Europe. The quantity of silver lace on the breeches varied according to rank. Ordinary troopers had all embroidery in white braid instead of silver; their sashes were green and orange. The post-October 1799 uniform is described in the body of the text.

B3 Fusiliers, 75me Demi-Brigade de Ligne, 1798–99
This shows the rear view of the cotton clothing and leather caps worn from October 1798 for the invasion of Syria. The buttons, which fastened the jacket down to the waist, were covered with blue cloth and the red turnbacks ended at the hip. Grenadiers had red epaulettes with a fringe. Secured to the upper part of the pouch belt and to a leather socket suspended from the pouch was a steel-tipped wooden pike fitted with chains; these were issued to each infantryman for Syria so that, when linked together and stuck in the ground, a *chevaux de frise* against cavalry could be formed. They were not a success and were discontinued after Syria. The cotton greatcoat is fastened to the knapsack with cords, since the latter had no straps for such a coat.

C1 Hussar, 7me bis Régiment de Hussards, 1799
This figure shows the clothing ordered for this regiment by the regulations of October 1799, with

The Battle of Aboukir, 1799; a rather fanciful engraving after Naudet, with the French infantry still in their 1798 uniforms. (Anna S. K. Brown Military Collection, Providence, Rhode Island)

the pelisse being worn over the dolman, of which the collar and cuffs were scarlet. The '*flamme*' of the mirliton is being worn with the black side outwards, as was customary in the field. The shoulder belt, worn over the dolman, suspended a black leather pouch and a carbine swivel. The flat braid bordering the yellow cords of the pelisse was repeated on the dolman. There is some evidence of scarlet breeches being worn, but possibly this was a privilege of the trumpeters. Sabretaches generally seem to have been scarlet with a lace border of the same colour as the braiding on the dolman and bore the Phrygian cap, fasces and the initials of the French Republic, but there were many regimental variations between 1792 and 1803.

C2 Officer, 18me Régiment de Dragons, 1799
Rear view of a field officer. The cuffs of this regiment were green with a rose-pink flap. For differences between this and the other regiments with pink facings (14th and 15th), see uniform section in body of text. Note the hussar boots introduced in June 1799. Officers below the rank of Major had a fringe only on the left epaulette, which

The 28th Foot fighting back to back at the Battle of Alexandria, the action for which they were granted their back badge. Painting by Lt-Col J. Marshman. (Reproduced by permission of The Gloucestershire Regiment)

were silver for all Dragoon officers. The sword is the 1790 model, as is that of the 3rd Dragoons figure.

C3 Chasseur, 22me Demi-Brigade Légère, 1798–99
Front view of the light infantry version of the cotton clothing. Fringed epaulettes were worn by all light infantry companies. *Carabiniers*, and grenadiers of the Line were distinguished by a grenade on both cap flaps. Unlike fusiliers, *chasseurs* carried a bayonet and *sabre-briquet* from the right shoulder belt.

D1 Drummer, 88me Demi-Brigade de Ligne, 1799–1801
Some demi-brigades clothed their drummers in reversed colours to those of the men, i.e. the red-coated 75th's drummers wore sky-blue faced red; but in the 88th they conformed with the remainder with the addition of green wings. The 88th was the only demi-brigade to have a lace loop on the collar, which was worn by all ranks. Unlike the cotton

coats which had the skirts turned back only in front, the coloured cloth coats had their skirts turned back front and rear, so that they fell over the hips. The pockets were set horizontally and had piping but no buttons. The coats of the 88th were originally ordered to be crimson but owing to cloth shortages they were issued with violet. Drummers were armed with a *sabre-briquet*.

D2 Field Officer, 4me Demi-Brigade Légère, 1799–1801

When the different coloured coats were introduced for the infantry in October 1799, officers adopted a *surtout* with long skirts in the same colours. Company officers wore trousers over hussar boots; these may have been the same colour as the men's, although the 9th Demi-Brigade wore green, a fashion possibly copied by others. In the Line, company officers appear to have carried their swords in a shoulder belt but for the light infantry a waistbelt with frog was more usual. Officially fusilier officers had a sword of the 1786 pattern with Republican modifications, while grenadier and light infantry company officers had sabres. Some adopted the more effective Mameluke weapons and in this, as in other aspects of officers' dress of this period, individual preferences were probably allowed considerable scope.

D3 Fusilier, 69me Demi-Brigade de Ligne, 1799–1801

The three demi-brigades illustrated on this page all played prominent parts in the main attack at Alexandria in 1801, dressed as shown, but the fourth unit of their division, the 18th, being dressed in red, were ordered to wear their shirts over their coats to avoid being confused with the British. According to A. Rigondaud's work on the 1799 coats, the four light demi-brigades and the 88th all had pointed cuffs, the remainder's being round. The method of suspending the bayonet from the pouch belt can be seen here, a practice that was followed by some grenadier companies for the sake of uniformity; the latter still continued to carry their sabres from a separate shoulder belt. Such items as water containers and haversacks were not an official issue in the French Army and had to be made up in Egypt.

Britain:

E1 Major-General, 1801

General officers at this period had three types of uniform: full dress, half dress or the embroidered coat, and undress or the plain coat – the latter is shown here. The collar was scarlet with a blue patch and a button at either end, and the coat could be worn with the blue lapels either buttoned back or buttoned over, as here. Rank was indicated by the gold-embroidered epaulettes with bullion fringe and the button spacing: generals having theirs regular, lieutenant-generals in threes, and major-generals in pairs. Note the round hat instead of the normal cocked hat.

E2 Private, Light Company, 28th (North Gloucestershire) Regiment of Foot, 1801

The lacquered black shako, about eight inches high, was introduced on 24 February 1800 to replace the hat. The worsted plume fitted behind a black leather cockade and brass button. The soldiers' coats had short skirts at the back, on which were placed the pocket flaps, each with four buttons and lace loops. The light companies' set on diagonally, the remainder horizontally. A lace diamond was sewn between the hip buttons where the back skirts joined. Wings were worn by the flank companies, the shoulder straps of the others ending in worsted tufts. The gaiters were secured by small white metal buttons and fastened to the breeches behind with a regimental button. This soldier is accoutred with his 60-round pouch and bayonet, both suspended by cross belts, and over his right shoulder is slung the haversack containing his provisions and a round wooden water bottle, painted blue. A General Order dated 6 March 1801 required the men's knapsacks to be left on board ship before the landing and only a blanket was carried, rolled and slung across the back. The battalion men's hair was queued but, in the flank companies, was plaited and turned up under the caps, with the ribbon hanging in three double loops and two single ends.

E3 Major, Corsican Rangers, 1801

The uniform shown here is taken from R. Ker Porter's painting of the death of Abercromby, which includes the figure of Hudson Lowe, then a major in the regiment. The front of the coat was

double-breasted, with black lapels which were usually worn buttoned over on service. The men wore the English shako with a silver bugle-horn and green plume. The collar and shoulder straps of their single-breasted jackets were edged with white lace, the straps ending in white worsted tufts, while the cuffs had three buttons with white lace loops. Their grey-blue pantaloons were worn with short black gaiters. All accoutrements were of black leather.

F1 Private, 12th (Prince of Wales's) Light Dragoons, 1801

On the right side of the helmet above the turban was the badge of the Prince of Wales's Feathers in white metal. The white braid round the bottom of the jacket continued round the back and up the seams, terminating in a knot. The silver braid on the officers' jackets was considerably more ornate (see illustration, p. 27). Hamilton Smith shows this regiment with buff breeches and belts, usually the prerogative of regiments with buff facings. At the start of the campaign, men of the 12th who were without horses were ordered to make over their carbines to the artillery and draw muskets and

Abercromby and his officers at Alexandria. The hatless mounted officer to the right of the colours is Moore; immediately below him, Major Wilson in the uniform of Hompesch's Mounted Rifles; at far left, moving right is Major Hudson Lowe, commanding the Corsican Rangers. Engraving after R. Ker Porter. (National Army Museum)

bayonets. The carbine swivel can be seen on the pouch belt. Note that the 12th's turbans were black, not of the facing colour.

F2 Officer, Grenadier Company, 58th (Rutlandshire) Regiment of Foot, 1801

This figure is based on a drawing made by William Loftie shortly after the regiment's return from Egypt. The white neck-cloth instead of the regulation black stock and the dark pantaloons with Hessian boots, rather than the prescribed white breeches and black gaiters (black-topped boots for field officers), were probably a personal preference for campaign wear. The red 'light' in the gold lace was a peculiarity of the 58th. The lapels of the double-breasted coat could be worn either as described for Figure E1 or as shown here. The white turn-backs were fastened with a grenade at the bottom of the long skirts, which had pockets set horizontally at hip level. As a flank company officer

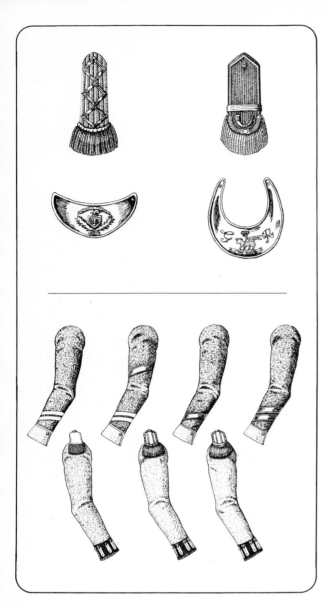

he wears an epaulette on both shoulders and small scarlet wings with fringes, sewn down to the sleeves under the epaulettes. Note the white plume of the grenadiers.

F3 Drummer, 40th (2nd Somerset) Regiment of Foot, 1801

The drummers' coats of all non-Royal regiments were in reversed colours and since the 40th were faced buff, his breeches and belts are of the same shade. All drummers wore bearskin caps with a black metal plate bearing the King's crest and trophies of colours and drums in brass, and can be seen so attired in de Loutherbourg's painting of the landing at Aboukir. Drummers' swords had a straight 24-inch blade with a hilt similar to the sergeants'. The 40th was represented in Egypt by the four flank companies of its two battalions, hence this man's hair is plaited and turned up under the cap in the manner prescribed, although drummers of all companies had their hair similarly dressed.

G1 Private, 90th (Perthshire Volunteers) Regiment of Foot, 1801

Since its formation in 1794 the 90th had been dressed and trained as light infantry, although not officially designated as such until 1815. At the Battle of Mandora their light dragoon helmets, with green plume and bugle-horn on the front of the fur crest, caused the French to mistake them for dismounted cavalry, with unfortunate results for the French Dragoons. The blue-grey pantaloons and half-gaiters had been worn since the formation, but their use in Egypt is less certain since an inspection report just after the campaign ended refers to 'buff breeches and long gaiters', although this may have been a badly-needed issue of new clothing. The brush and picker for cleaning the musket lock were worn hanging from the belt plate, which was brass and oval.

G2 Sergeant, Battalion Company, 3rd Foot Guards, 1801

This figure shows the rear of the other ranks' infantry coat, although the gold lace was peculiar to Foot Guards sergeants. The front of this NCO's coat had gold lace vertically down the opening and nine buttons in threes with gold lace loops, each three inches long with pointed ends; the cuffs and pocket flaps also had only three buttons. A gold-

Officers' rank distinctions. *Left:* French lieutenant's epaulette and gorget (25me Demi-Brigade). Colonels had fringe on both straps, junior ranks on left strap only. Gold (Line) or silver (Light Infantry) lace for Colonels, Chefs de Bataillon, and Captains. Lieutenants had flame-coloured silk embroidery on the lace, Sous-Lieutenants one epaulette only, the reverse of Lieutenants. *Right:* British epaulette (90th Foot) and gorget (2nd Foot). Epaulettes of gold or silver according to regimental lace, worn on both shoulders by field officers and flank company officers, on right shoulder only by remainder. No variations between ranks but many differences of detail between regiments. (Author's sketches)

NCOs' rank distinctions. *Top, l. to r:* French, on both arms – Corporal (matching piping); Fourrier (lower as piping, upper as buttons); Sergeant; Sergeant-Major (both matching buttons). *Bottom, l. to r:* British, right shoulder only – Corporal (white lace strap and worsted fringe); Sergeant (silver lace strap with two red stripes, twisted red and silver cord around, silver fringe); Sergeant-Major (as Sergeant but with silver crescent). Colours varied in some regiments. (Author's sketches)

Three typical French infantrymen in 1798 regarding a small Sphinx. Lithograph after H. Bellange. (National Army Museum)

laced epaulette with fringe was worn on the right shoulder to denote rank in the battalion companies, and on both by the flank companies, over gold-laced and fringed blue wings. The Coldstream coats were similar but with 10 buttons in front in pairs and four on the cuffs and pockets; their sashes were plain crimson. White lace for the men in both regiments. This sergeant wears the back flap of his shako down, a battalion company plume, and hair queued according to regulations. The white undress trousers are worn to protect the breeches. The nine-foot pike was carried by all grenadier and battalion sergeants, those of the light company having fusils. Brass-hilted sword.

G3 Private, Hompesch's Mounted Rifles, 1801
The half-lapels of this jacket were popular with the foreign regiments, being also worn by Löwenstein's and the *Chasseurs Britanniques*. The right shoulder belt suspended the sword from slings and the left a black pouch and carbine swivel. The officers'

uniform was more ornate having a gold-laced scarlet shako, slightly wider at the top, with detachable peak, gold cap lines, and tall white plume with black top; the scarlet lapels continued to the waist, each with a row of gilt buttons and horizontal T-shaped gold loops; gold lace on the collar, cuffs and breeches; gold and crimson piping on the sleeve and back seams; gold epaulettes and crimson sash; black leather pouch belt with gilt studs and edging; crimson Russia leather waistbelt and slings, and black sabretache (see illustration, p. 35).

H1 Gunner, Royal Artillery, 1801
The Foot Artillery's shako plate was of a slightly different shape from the infantry's, having concave sides. Although by 1815 their coats had eight buttons in front, at this period there were only five.

The short skirts at the rear had horizontal pockets and only three buttons. The two prickers and hammer for clearing the vent and the red flask cord can be seen on the left shoulder belt, the flask itself resting on the white pouch behind (see the gunner in the illustration on p. 29). Although the gunner's personal weapons consisted of musket and bayonet, there is evidence of some carrying brass-hilted hangers, as here, perhaps when serving the guns.

H2 Sergeant-Major, 92nd (Highland) Regiment of Foot, 1801

A regimental order dated 7 March 1799 stated that the bonnets of the men were to have 'one large feather, six small and one hackle' and in 1800 it was further ordered that the whole headdress was to be 15 inches in height. Highlanders' coats had only eight buttons in front and three on the pockets, which sloped diagonally. Sergeants were distinguished by scarlet, not red, coats; plain white lace (possibly silver for the sergeant-major); a sash with a stripe of the facing colour, which was worn over the left shoulder only by Highlanders; and an epaulette on the right shoulder, its design being usually a regimental decision. The 92nd's kilts were of the Government tartan with a yellow line. Sporrans were not worn in the field. A regimental order dated 23 September 1800 required the men to have half-gaiters made up, and there is some evidence that before landing in Egypt the regiment had leather peaks fixed to their bonnets. Whether the sergeant-major carried a sergeant's pike is uncertain; this man has an NCO's broadsword and drill sergeant's cane.

H3 Private, Battalion Company, de Watteville's Swiss Regiment, 1801

De Watteville's was formed for Mediterranean service from four Swiss regiments in British pay which had been fighting alongside the Austrians. On its arrival in Malta in July 1801, it received uniforms brought from Germany which had been made for one of the Swiss corps, Rovéréa's. In 1803 it was dressed as British infantry. In 1801 it had a *chasseur* company, distinguished by a dark green plume and edging to the turban, black belts, a hide-covered pack slung *en banderole* with a white strap, and a sword bayonet. Much of the equipment seems to have come from Austrian sources, including the greatcoat, the Hungarian pantaloons, accoutrements and weapons. The officers wore a bicorne with feather according to their company; a green *surtout* with black collar, cuffs and linings; gilt buttons and epaulette on the right shoulder; green waistcoat with two rows of gilt buttons; blue Hungarian pantaloons and short boots; white sword belt with slings.

SELECT BIBLIOGRAPHY

Brunon, Raoul and Jean. *Garde Impériale – Mameluks*, Marseilles, n.d.

Chandler, David. *The Campaigns of Napoleon*, London, 1967.

Fortescue, Sir John. *A History of the British Army* (Vol. IV), London, 1899–1930.

Guitry, Commandant(ed.). *L'Armée de Bonaparte 1798–99*, Paris, 1897.

Herold, J. Christopher. *Bonaparte in Egypt*, London, 1963.

Jonquière, C. de la. *L'Expédition d'Égypte 1798–1801*, 5 vols., Paris, n.d.

Oman, Carola. *Sir John Moore*, London, 1953.

Phipps, R. W. *Armies of the First French Republic*, London, 1939.

Reynier, General. *Memoires II – Campagne d'Égypte*, Paris, 1827.

Walsh, Thomas. *Journal of the late Campaign in Egypt*, London, 1803.

Wilson, Robert. *History of the British Expedition to Egypt*, London, 1803.

Uniforms

Carman, W. Y. (ed.). *Infantry Clothing Regulations 1802*, Journal of S.A.H.R. Vol. XIX, 1940.

Grouvel, Vicomte. *Les Corps de Troupe de l'Émigration Française*, Paris, 1957

Lawson, C. C. P. *A History of the Uniforms of the British Army*, (Vols. III–V), London, 1961–67.

Lienhart and Humbert, *L'Uniforme de l'Armée Française*, 5 vols., Paris, 1897.

Reynolds, P. W. (MSS). *Military Costume of the 18th and 19th Centuries*, Vols. VIII–XI, LVI.

Rigondaud, Albert. *Les Extraordinaires Tenues de l'Armée d'Orient*, Gazette des Uniformes, 1975–76.

Types of the British forces in Egypt with medallions of senior officers. *From top, clockwise:* Seaman; Light Dragoon; Marine; Light Dragoon; Grenadier, Foot Guards; Royal Artillery; Minorca Regiment; 42nd Highlanders; Sepoy. The mounted figure is a Turk or Mameluke. Engraving after P. J. de Loutherbourg. (National Army Museum)

Notes sur les planches en couleur

A1 Dragon, 3e Régiment de Dragons, 1798. Prenez note de distinctions en forme de manchettes, poches et basques. Pantalons et bottes à la mode d'hussard remplacèrent les culottes et les bottes illustrées de juin 1799. Crinière ne fut pas portée en combat. **A2** Général de Division français 1798, de portraits de Kléber et Desaix. Variations de crinière et de ceinture distinguantes censément de grades différents de général ne sont pas crues avoir été rigidement observées. **A3** Grenadier, 18e Demi-Brigade de Ligne, 1798, les épaulettes rouges et la crinière filante distinguantes un grenadier. Les pantalons rayés, 'pantalons de route', furent distribués à Toulens et aux 25e, 32e et 75e Demi-Brigades. Prenez note de calot sous cartouchière, et sabre-briquet de grenadier.

B1 Carabinier, 21e Demi-Brigade Légère, 1798–99; comme partie de la division de Desaix, cette fraction n'eut pas reçu tenues de cotonnade et les tenues européenes deteriorèrent rapidement. **B2** Officier, 22e Régiment de Chasseurs à Cheval, 1798. Soldats ordinaires tinrent galon blanc au lieu de l'argentée et ceintures vertes-et-orangées. On croit que la fraction complète porta le chapeau bicorne. **B3** Fusiliers, 75e Demi-Brigade de Ligne, 1798–99, mis en les tenues de cotonnade et les casquettes de cuir utilisées dans l'invasion de la Syrie. Prenez note de jalons en bois avec ferrures d'acier distribués pour cette campagne afin que l'infanterie pût se former chevaux-de-frise contre assaut de cavalerie.

C1 Hussard, 7e bis Régiment de Hussards, mis en tenue consignée par réglements d'octobre 1799. La flamme du chapeau mirliton est portée avec le côté noir à l'exterieur quand en campagne. **C2** Officier le plus élevé en grade, 18e Régiment de Dragons, 1799, montrant distinctions du régiment à manchette, à poche et aux basques. Officiers qui ne furent pas si plus élevés en grade comme chef de bataillon tinrent une frange seulement sur l'épaulette gauche. **C3** Chasseur, 22e Demi-Brigade Légère, 1798–99, mis en la version de l'infanterie légère de la tenue de cotonnade—toutes compagnies de fraction d'infanterie légère portèrent épaulettes mais carabiniers portèrent un écusson d'une grenade sur la casquette.

D1 Tambour, 88e Demi-Brigade de Ligne, 1799–1801; quelques fractions habillèrent leurs tambours en couleurs renversées mais la 88e ajouta tout bonnement ailes vertes aux épaules. Dans toute cette fraction fut portée une bride de dentelle sur le col—un trait unique. **D2** Officier le plus élevé en grade, 4e Demi-Brigade Légère, 1799–1801, portant le surtout en couleurs de régiment. Officiers d'infanterie légère portèrent ordinairement le ceinturon à la ceinture, tandis que dans les fractions de ligne un baudrier fût plus ordinaire. **D3** Fusilier, 69e Demi-Brigade de Ligne, 1799–1801, et variation typiques de casquettes et de 'pouffes'.

E1 Major-General anglais mis en la tunique sans dessin et sans dentelle d'or, favorisée en campagne, avec le chapeau à larges bords remplaçant le chapeau bicorne ordinaire chaud au climat chaud. Generals tinrent boutons que furent bien espacés, et Lieutenant-Generals tinrent boutons par trois. **E2** Le shako fut introduit en février 1800. Infanterie Légère et compagnies de grenadiers portèrent 'ailes' sur la tunique. Une consigne de mars 1801 décréta que l'Havresack fut être laissé à bord et la couverture mise en bandoulière sur le dos du soldat. **E3** Major, Corsican Rangers, d'un tableau de Hudson Lowe quand il fut officier dans cette fraction. Les revers noires de cette tunique furent d'habitude boutonnés clos quand en campagne. Les soldats portèrent dentelle blanche sur la tunique et un shako anglais avec un écusson argenté d'un clairon et un pompon vert.

F1 Les ailes sur les épaulettes identifient un des grenadiers ou l'infanterie légère. Le foulard, les pantalons et les bottes furent probablement affaires de goût. La ligne rouge dans la dentelle d'or fut une singularité de la 58th Foot. **F2** Comme tambour d'un régiment—40th Foot—sans mot 'Royal', il porte une tunique de la couleur du parement du régiment, parée rouge. Fractions avec parements de couleur chamois, comme ici, portèrent aussi culottes et ceintures de couleur chamois. Soldats de compagnies flank portèrent les cheveux à tresses et retroussés sous le shako au lieu de les portant dans un queue; la 40th Foot fut seulement représentée en Égypte par les compagnies flank de ses deux bataillons. **F3** Dragons de la 12th portèrent dentelle blanche, officiers portèrent argentée. L'écusson du Prince of Wales fut porté sur le côté droit du casque.

G1 La 90th Foot fut employée comme infanterie légère; leurs tenues portèrent les Français à les prendre pour la cavalerie démontée avec résultats mortels. Il est possible qu'ils portèrent culottes de couleur chamois et longues guêtres noires au lieu de celles-là illustrées ici. **G2** Le dos d'une tunique de soldat montrant par un sergent de Guards; mais prenez note de la dentelle d'or qui fut un privilège de sous-officiers de Guards, et soldats ordinaires portèrent dentelle blanche. Ce sergent tiendrait dentelle d'or sur le devant de la tunique, et neuf brides de dentelle des boutons arrangées par trois. Piques furent portées par sergents de compagnies de grenadier et battalion, fusils légers de sergents à compagnie de light-infantry. **G3** Ce soldat de Hompesch's Mounted Rifles porte une tunique avec les revers de demi-longueur qui furent en vogue dans corps étranger en arme britannique.

H1 À cette période la tunique de soldat de Royal Artillery tint seulement cinq boutons. Deux prickers et un marteau furent portés sur la ceinture-croix et la corde rouge supporta une poire à poudre qui fut suspendue en haut de la cartouchière au derrière de la hanche. **H2** Les particularités de tenue Highland portée ici par un sergeant-major de la 92nd Foot. La ceinture fut portée autour de l'épaule seulement par fractions Highland; ici, l'épaulette sur l'épaule droite fut de dessin de régiment. Le sporran ne fut pas porté en campagne. **H3** de Watteville's Regiment fut composé des soldats de quatre régiments suisse à la solde britannique et il porta la tenue d'un d'eux, Rovéréa's Regiment. Beaucoup d'équipement autrichien fut employé.

Farbtafeln

A1 Dragoner, 3e Régiment de Dragons, 1798. Bemerken Regimentsunterscheidungen in der Erscheinungsform Stulpen, Taschen und Rockschösse. Beinkleid und Stiefel in der Mode Husars haben von Juni 1799 die Stelle der illustrierten Reithosen und Stiefel eingenommen. Der Federbusch wurde nicht im Gefecht getragen. **A2** Französischer Général de Division 1798 von Porträten Klébers und Desaix. Veränderungen Federbusches und Leibbinde unterschiedeten vermutlich von verschiedenen Graden Generals aber man glaubt, dass diese nicht streng beachtet wurden. **A3** Grenadier, 18e Demi-Brigade de Ligne, 1798, die rote Epauletten und der Fallenfederbusch unterscheiden einen Grenadier. Die gestreifte Hosen, 'pantalons de route', wurde zu diesem Verband und zu den 25e, 32e und 75e Demi-Brigades in Toulon ausgegeben. Bemerken die Feldmütze unter Patronentasche und sabre-briquet Grenadiers.

B1 Carabinier, 21e Demi-Brigade Légère, 1798–99; als einen Teil der Division Desaixs hat dieser Verband keine Baumwolluniformen bekommen und Europäische Uniformen verschlechterten sich schnell. **B2** Offizier, 22e Régiment de Chasseurs à Cheval, 1798. Gemeine Soldaten besassen weisse Schnur anstatt die Silbere, und grüne und orangefarbige Leibbinden. Es ist gedacht, dass der ganze Verband den Bicorne-Hut trug. **B3** Fusiliers, 75e Demi-Brigade de Ligne, 1798–99, auf den Baumwolluniformen und Mützen aus Leder bekleidet, die in dem Einfall in Syrien eingesetzt wurden. Bemerken Pfähle aus Holz mit Zubehören aus Stahl, die für diesen Feldzug ausgegeben wurden, so dass Infanterie chevaux-de-frise gegen Reiterei-angriff formieren konnte.

C1 Husar, 7e bis Régiment de Hussards, in Uniform von den Verordnungen Oktobers 1799 befohlen. Die mirliton Huts ist mit der schwarzen Seite auswärts getragen, wenn man ins Feld rückt. **C2** Oberoffizier, 18e Régiment de Dragons, 1799, der Regimentsunterscheidungen an Stulpe, Tasche und Rockschoss trägt. Offiziere unter dem Dienstgrad Majors trugen eine Franse nur auf der linken Épaulette. **C3** Chasseur, 22e Demi-Brigade Légère, 1798–99, auf der Version leichter Infanterie der Baumwolluniform—alle Kompagnien leichter Infanterieabteilungen trugen Epauletten.

D1 Trommler, 88e Demi-Brigade de Ligne, 1799–1801; einige Abteilungen kleideten ihren Trommlers in umgekehrten Farben aber die 88e tan einfach grüne Flugzeugführerabzeichen auf den Achseln hinzu. Diese Abteilung trug ganz und gar eine Öse aus Spitze am Kragen—ein einzigartiges Kennzeichen. **D2** Oberoffiziere, 4e Demi-Brigade Légère, 1799–1801, auf dem surtout in Regimentsfarben bekleidet. Offiziere leichter Infanterie trugen gewöhnlich das Degengehenk am Bund, während eines Schultergehenk in den Abteilungen vordester Stellung viel gewöhnlicher getragen wurde. **D3** Fusilier, 69e Demi-Brigade de Ligne, 1798–1801, und typische Abänderungen Mützen und 'pouffes'.

E1 Englischer Major-General auf dem einfarbigen Rock ohne goldene Spitze bekleidet, dem im Feldzug vorgezogen wurde, mit einem breitrandigem Hut, dem der übliche Bicorne-Hut in diesem warmen Klima ersass. Generals besassen Knöpfe, die in regelmässigen Zwischenräumen angeordnet wurden, und Lieutenant-Generals besassen Knöpfe zu dreien. **E2** Der Tschako wurde in Februar 1800 aufgebracht. Leichte Infanterie und Kompagnien Grenadiers trugen Flugzeugführerabzeichen auf dem Waffenrock. Die Aufstellung März 1801 ordnete an, dass der Tornister an Bord Schiff zurückgelassen wurde und die Wolldecke von der Schulter gehängt. **E3** Major, Corsican Rangers, von einem Gemälde Hudson Lowes, als er Offizier dieser Abteilung war. Wenn in Kampfe wurden die schwarze Aufschläge des Rocks gewöhnlich zugeknöpft. Die Soldaten trugen weisse Spitze auf dem Rock und einen englischen Tschako mit einem silbernen Signalhorns und grüne Troddel.

F1 Die Flugzeugführerabzeichen unter den Epauletten identifizieren einen Offizier Grenadiers oder leichte Infanterie. Das Halstuch, die Beinkleider und Stiefel waren aller Wahrscheinlichkeit nach eine persönliche Geschmackssache. Die rote Linie in der goldenen Spitze war eine Eigentümlichkeit der 58th Foot. **F2** Als Trommler eines Regiments—40th Foot—ohne 'Royal' Zustand trägt er einen Rock in der Besatzfarbe des Regiments, auf rot gesetzt. Abteilungen mit ledergelben Besätzen, wie man hier illustriert hat, trugen auch ledergelbe Kniehosen und Gürtel. Soldaten Flank Kompagnien trugen die Haare geflecht und unter dem Tschako getragen, statt sie in einem Zopf zu tragen; die 40th Foot wurde nur die Flank-Kompagnien seiner zwei Batallions in Ägypten vertretet. **F3** Dragoner der 12ten trugen weisse Spitze, Offiziere trugen silbere.

G1 Die 90th Foot wurde als leichte Infanterie angestellt. Ihre Uniform brachte die Fanzösen sie für abgessene Kavallerie mit tödlichen Folgen zu verwechseln. Es ist möglich, dass sie ledergelbe Reithosen und hohe schwarze Gamaschen trügen, statt dieser hier illustriert. **G2** Der Rücken des Rocks eines Soldats von einem Guards Unteroffizier getragen—aber bemerken, dass die goldene Spitze ein Vorrecht Guards Unteroffiziers war und gemeine Soldaten trugen weisse Spitze. Dieser Unteroffizier würde goldene Spitze auf dem Einsatz des Rocks und neun Ösen von den Knöpfen zu dreien angeordnet besitzen. Spiesse wurden von Unteroffizieren grenadier und battalion Kompagnien getragen, leichte fusils von Kompagnienunteroffizieren light-infantry Kompagnie. **G3** Dieser Soldat Hompesch's Mounted Rifles trägt einen Rock mit den Aufschlägen halben Länge.

H1 An dieser Zeit besass der Rock eines Soldats Royal Artillery nur fünf Knöpfe. Zwei prickers und ein Hammer wurden auf dem Quergürtel getragen und die rote Schnur trug ein für abgessene Kavallerie in Pulverfeldflasche, die ober der Patronentasche hinter der Hüfte hängte auf. **H2** Die Eigenheiten Highland uniform von einem sergeant-major der 92nd Foot hier getragen. Die Leibbinde wurde nur von Highlandverbände ringsum der Schulter getragen; hier, die Epaulette auf der rechten Schulter war Regimentsmuster. Die sporran wurden nicht im Feldzug getragen. **H3** De Watteville's Regiment wurde von Soldaten vier Schweizregiments in britische Sold ausgemacht und sie trugen die vorige Uniform eines der Vier, Rovéréa's Regiment. Viele österreichische Ausrüstung wurde eingesetzt.